Becoming

My Personal Memoirs

Lacresha N. Hayes

Living Waters Publishing Company
Marion, AR

Becoming: My Personal Memoirs
(Formerly printed under the title *Whispers of the Heart*

ISBN: 978-0-9798154-3-0

LCCN: 2007907757

Published by Living Waters Publishing Company
Arkansas, Louisiana and Tennessee
www.livingwaterspc.com

Printed in United States

Other Books by the Author

The Rape of Innocence: Taking Captivity Captive

Christian Principles Series:
My Thoughts Exactly
Walk With Me

Introducing the Culpeppers

A Culpepper Easter

Soon to be Released:

From the Christian Principles Series
All or Nothing
Heavenly Voices
Manifested Promises

The Culpepper Vacation

Simplistic Choices

Full Exposure

Acknowledgments

I would like to acknowledge my late grandmother, Annie L. Hardaway. She taught me to stand under pressure, no matter how great. I also want to acknowledge my mother whose poetic gift used to wow me. She is still the best poet I've ever had the pleasure to read from.

There are so many others who believed in me and pushed me forward when I wanted to stop. I thank you all and appreciate your efforts.

Introduction

For me, writing has been a very personal journey. It has helped me face the worst of times with an outlet of expression. Writing has been therapeutic through deaths in my family, bad health and very little money. Through bad relationships and faltering faith, God gave me poetry to help me re-gain my perspective.

As I sat alone one night, I thought about all the people who have been through and will go through the same things I have been through in life. I thought of the many people who lack the outlet I have; those who feel alone in their circumstances. I thought of you. My testimony is not mine alone, but it belongs to all those who read this, my journal. My life is now literally an open book. My thoughts and emotions are out in the open for everyone to see and judge. Yet, I make the decision to publish my personal memoirs. I can't help but feel some trepidation. I can't help but wonder if these accounts set to poetry are enough to minister to someone. They minister to me even now. They hold all my raw and unbridled emotions. They reflect the face of a woman who was becoming.

As I compose this book of the poetry of my heart, I look back and find solace and comfort in my Christ. I realize even more that He was always there, and even now is still with me. I find Him to be who He says He is - a very present help in trouble. He was a shelter, though at times I felt completely exposed. He was a refuge, though many times I felt all alone, and lost, and rejected, and forsaken. Yet, I was never forsaken. Will you understand that as you read? Time will tell.

I pray that you come to a place that Christ is everything to you. Nothing else works. Here is my story. Read it and come to your own conclusion.

Act 1

Lost in My Pain

Little Girl Lost

Alone in the world
Stands a lost little girl
Where can she run in the night?
Being tossed in every known direction
She stands unguarded with no protection
She just sits there and trembles in fright

Who has seen this poor girl's affliction?
Who has even cared?
Who has given her well-deserved attention?
Or shown her a love that's shared?

No one cares about the trouble she's known
No one seems to look
Though her body is full grown
Her mind still needs to be shook

Everyone she loves has used her
Her own family has abused her
Who could this little girl be?
Look in the mirror. Who do you see?

Every woman has a little girl lost
Though not all of them paid the same cost

The Mirage

When you look at me
What do you see
Can you see the scars inside
Can you tell I cry
Sometimes want to die
A woman too full of pride

Can you see the tears
Shed over the years
Or do you only see my shell
Can you see past my smile
Tell it's fake from a mile
Or do you believe all is well

If you knew me really
Would you think me silly
Because love is all I crave
If you knew my heart
Would it give you a start
To find out it's an empty cave

When you look at me
Tell me, what you see

Nobody's Baby

The curve of my body awakens my senses
The softness of my skin seems to entice
The flow of my hair tells a story
The fullness of my lips speak it softly
I am nobody's baby

The emotions of life begin in me
Thinking I know what love is
Experiencing what must be passion
Enjoying the newness of an awakened flame
I am nobody's baby

A broken heart tells the story
All the confusion and lies that came in
The man of my dreams with another woman
My emotions left in total upheaval
It all seems to speak; I am nobody's baby

Wish I were still a baby
And had my mother to comfort me
But growing up fast only proved
Nobody's baby is yet a baby still!

All Alone

To the father I knew too little about

Where is the one who should love me?
Oh, how I've sought him, where could he be?
Where is this love every little girl needs?
I keep seeking while my heart bleeds

Who will protect me when I'm down?
There is no one to be found
Who will lift me up when I fall?
I have no one that I can call
Does anyone care about my life?
How it's filled with doubt and strife
Am I made of cellophane?
Or to really look at me does that bring you pain?

I need someone because I'm human too
Maybe you didn't know that, but it's true
I am beautiful and I am smart
Just look and you'll see
I deserve to be in your heart
A space reserved only for me
All of a sudden you're dead, you're gone
I'm by myself and left all alone!

Suicide

Death of my thoughts
Death of my wishes
Life has me caught
Between two decisions

Not wanting to stay here
But don't know where to go
Feel like change is so near
But good things come so slow

What do I do
Which road do I take
Wish those around me knew
But, what difference would it make

Lord, let me die
This is my dream
All I do is cry
Things are worse than they seem

Help me, Lord
Please do it Master
I'm at the end of my cord
On the verge of disaster

Regulate My Mind

Memories, how do they go away
What do you do when they want to stay

How can you forget his lips
His lips all over you
How can you forget that smile
That smile that pierced right through you

Trying to forget him
The way he held my hand
Trying to move beyond him
Make room for a new man

Somehow, I seem to be stuck
Even with all the prayer
Still I desire to see him
Knowing he doesn't care

My mind is gone, at the point of obsession
Is there any help for me
My food and drink are depression
The thoughts won't let me be

So, I run back to God, seeking His face
A lady once told me that He was full of grace
She said He had authority over everything
All I had to do was grab hold and cling
She said that he was powerful and kind
Able also to regulate my mind

Leave No Doubts

Will you keep your promises?
You made them so long ago
Can I count on your Word?
Or do I lean on what I know?

Is there anyone who can help me?
Lead me to a safer place
Is there someone I can trust in?
Someone to encourage me in this race

Can you keep my heart?
Make me to be whole
Can you give me peace?
Put a joy down in my soul

Is it true you're all powerful?
Creator of everything
Can you make mountains bow down?
Are you the reason birds sing?

If you can do all this and more
Snap your fingers, help me out
If you can do the impossible
Show yourself, leave no doubts!

Act 2

Meeting My Savior

A Love Story

The greatest love of my life, my Savior, Jesus Christ

The dew of the morning glistens
It tells the story of the night before
His aroma still seems to linger
His voice can still be heard
The touch of his hand can still be felt

As the moon becomes radiant
So does His love for me
He holds me closer to him
He comforts me until sleep takes control
And in the morning, He is still there

Love professed is often weak
How can words ever describe my love for Him
It overruns the spectrum of emotions
It floods the pits of my soul

Nothing in all creation is so precious
Nothing in creation as powerful
As the bond between two lovers
The bond between me and my God

Jesus, All Mine

The blessing of the Lord makes you rich
It never adds any sorrow
Because Christ is on the throne
You don't have to worry about tomorrow

In His presence is fullness of joy
He has given us things here to enjoy

Because of Him we can do anything
It's all by His power
He gives us a new song to sing
He is our strong tower

How I love Jesus
The sweetest name I will ever know
How my soul longs for Him
I carry His presence wherever I go
There is none like Him in my eyes
Anything in comparison would be despised

Still, I know my shepherd's voice
He talks to me all the time
Everyday I make the choice
To let Him be all mine

The Potter

As I look down through the years
At all those days so full of tears
I can't help but remember who mended me
Who put everything where it should be

Though my choices sometimes made it hard
Often I played the wrong card
It was only the Potter who could mend
All the things I decided to rend

It was my decisions that hurt so deep
That kept me up at night, unable to sleep
But by his loving hands, he healed me
The Potter showed his love for me

He relieved my guilt, removing my shame
Erasing my doubts, demolishing my blame
He wiped away every tear
Bottled it and kept it near

He washed away all my sin
God put me back together again

Take Me Easy

Gently you whisper my name
Repeatedly you speak
Because of you, I'll never be the same
By your voice, my knees go weak

Softly you speak to my heart
I begin to quiver
You promise me a brand new start
And even though I shiver
You always take me easy

You show me a glimpse of a future so bright
But you do it ever so sweetly
Flooding me with the softest light
Overwhelming my senses completely
Because I may not always understand
You continue to take me easy

You passionately lead me to unseen lands
Guiding me always with your eye
Keeping me perpetually in your hands
All I can do is cry
As a suave suitor, you breathe my name
With a persuasion to trust you more
Because of you, I will never be the same
You've penetrated my very core

As your glory rises upon me
And I hear your voice in my ear
I whisper back to you
"Please, Lord, take me easy!"

The Fabric

Nothing about me is what they expected
I'm cut from a different cloth, he said
I'm not basic black nor true blue
But my heart beats blood red

My mind is fixed on pleasing God
My heart is full of HIS decrees
I'm here only for HIS purposes
I have to do HIS will, even if no one agrees

The tapestry of destiny is apparent in my life
And by God's providential hand
When my season is over, I will have left promise
One day you will understand

The separation that occurred at the right time
Was determined before you were made
Now, I return to my Father
The plans has already been laid

The fabric of my being I leave with you
As the days go on, what will you do

Conversion

What is it I may give to you
What, indeed, could I render
Is there something I can present to you
Or is there something I can do
While my heart beats only for you

You see me naked, through and through
All things in life are bare to you
Yet you love with an everlasting love
Yet, you bless with unshaken mercy
In spite of my flaws, your love isn't affected at all

You have become my very heart's desire
You are truly all I need
In you I find hope for the future
Joy to carry on
Peace to calm my troubled mind

Yes, I'm yours in all that I am
Unequivocally so
No one has ever loved me like you do
And there's no one I love more than you
You are my personal God
You belong to me
I am your personal child
For as long as you'll have me

The Late Night Creep

Moonlight and stars make the night
The atmosphere feels just right
Everyone in my house is asleep
It's so quiet, you can't hear a peep

I ease out the door, making no sound
Looking for a place where I can kneel down
And make my requests known unto Him
Realizing this night I really need Him

He knows the truth, whether or not I lie
With Him there is nothing that gets by
So I cast upon Him all my cares
Assured in my heart He hears my prayers

And knowing that He stands so near
I have no reason to be filled with fear
Though my life isn't all that great
It's nothing He can't fix if only I wait

So tonight, I wait no matter how it seems
Knowing only Jesus can fulfill my dreams

He Heard My Cry

Oh, how I love him
The man of my dreams
I think so much of him
He fulfills all my needs

He's always there
He never takes a rest
He is everywhere
He loves me best

God, your Son is wonderful to me
Everything about him makes me happy
Jesus, how I love that name
He takes good care of me
Thank God He always stays the same
He doesn't change on me

Joy fills my heart
Tears fill my eyes
Sorrow disappears
Love starts to rise

I love the Lord
He did indeed hear my cry

God's Love

My life is a testimony to His greatness
There was nothing wonderful about me
But in His infinite mercy He found
Something in me He could use

Bringing me out of my misery
He was the lifter of my head
He stabilized my life
And made me a witness to man

In my destitution
He gave me a reason to believe
He redeemed me from my past
And set me on higher ground

In all my shame, He chose me still
He designed a path for me to walk
Not that I deserved it, but He's given me life
All because He loves me

A Needful Thing

It's a needful thing for your heart to sing
Though this world can bring you down
People are contrary, yet it's necessary
For us to keep them around

It's a needful thing to quite often bring
All your worries to God in prayer
No matter what you do, He's listening to you
Peeling away that troubled layer

Love is a needful thing
When you find it, your mouth can sing
Of the mercy found at the cross
And the goodness that kept us from being lost

Faith is a needful thing
Without it we have no wing
To fly away from sorrow and care
And give Jesus our burdens so He can bear

What do you think when life starts to sing
I remember God is a needful thing

The Christ

It was Christ
Who paid the price
For me to be whole
He had to cry
And then to die
To redeem my soul

Once He entered into my heart
I became a major part
Of His perfect plan
He healed me
And set me free
As a testimony to man

God sent His best when He sent His Son
When He bowed His head, the works were done
"If I be lifted up, I'll draw all men to me"
The perfect plan of God we could not see

It was Christ who made a new and living way
For us to come to the Father every day
For this I thank Him and praise His name
If we don't accept Him, we still have blame

Act 3

Troubled by my Flesh

What Is Human

A love lost
A dream tossed
A house divided
Everything seems one-sided

But through it all, I hang tough
Though my life seems so rough
God has given me what it takes
I have to make it for other's sake

I have destiny wrapped up in me
And there is so much I need to be
But just the same, I get weak
Sometimes I find I'm unable to speak

I find that I'm not satisfied
And with all my success, I can't be gratified
I find myself feeling all alone
Without even a friend that I can phone

And with all the people who are around
It only makes me feel like I'm bound
So I seek to be set free
Jesus, have your way in me

Let me soar above my human side
And forget all the long nights I've cried
In all that I find to do
I will trust only in you

Mind Games Before the Honeymoon

Was it his way of talking to me
Or was I only blind
To the sweet things he said to me
Knowing he was playing with my mind

Was I really taken by this man
Or was it in my head
Is there something special about his hand
Or was it in something he said

There is now no way to know
How this thing is going to go
But in it all, I often ask
Is he really worth the task

Could it be I'm playing the fool for him
I never tell him no
Am I possibly falling in love with him
Turning away from all I know

Reading the Bible is one thing
Acting it out is another
It feels right since I wear his ring
Isn't it if we love each other

His mind games have me confused
Yet, I refuse to walk away
I know my body is being abused
Still I choose to stay

Reality

You never really knew
How I felt about you
We just went through the motion
Never did you see
The most sensitive side of me
Your heart never had the notion

To you it was a game
It was just the same
As it had been so many times before
I had given my love in vain
I was feeling the pain
It was destroying my very core

Would you do it different now
That you know how
Your playing and lies hurt me
Or would you do it in spite
Bedding me tonight
Knowing that you don't want me

In this reality that I must face
In your heart I have no place
You're not mine, what can I say
I can only go on my way

Days Gone By

Leaves fall from the trees
The streets once beautiful are now dull
Autumn has come, summer is gone
So much like the life I once had

No worries, no pain, no stress
As the wind blows softly through my hair
I reflect back to days of peace
I look at the perfectly orange sky

The sun sets below my dreams
How I wish for days gone by
Long gone is the time of rocking chairs
The era of lawn furniture is dead

Times of the slip and slide have disappeared
Now only fast cars and fast food survive
No more rest and relaxation
Only rush hour traffic and tardiness

No more comfort in your arms
I only have your picture and your shirt
I only have the memories of days gone by
But I should have you

It

We talked for hours
Weather, sports, food
We hummed and sang
Tunes of yester year
But not once did we speak of it
It was so long ago
It was in times past
Today was a new day
And we would rather laugh at birds
Wade in streams
Throw rocks at tree barks
But no mention of it
It would only complicate things
It is a distant sound on the seashore
It is a wake up call from a rooster not yours
Look at the sky, why is it blue
And other such nonsense
All in an effort to leave it behind
It is just a thought in the back of our minds
But never will we speak of it

Never Satisfied

It seems I'm never satisfied
I can never get enough
My soul is never gratified
My spirit has it rough
Though the Lord I do confess
My life somehow is still a mess

I can never seem to escape my past
And in all things I finish last
Found a love, but it wasn't right
Still in darkness though I've seen the light

Can the imprisoned set themselves free
Can the lost be found
Will the blind man ever see
Can the shackled be unbound

Can my future be prophesied
And I be told what my tomorrows hold
I say we are never satisfied
That's the truth, big and bold!

Fallen of God's Best

I often feel sorrow in my heart
Looking at the fallen of God's best
You and I
The fallen of God's best

How long will we torment Him
Playing games with His heart
We never stop long enough to say, "Thank you!"
We go about our lives until hell breaks out

We go on with our sin, heads in the clouds
We hurt ourselves, yet blame others
When it was our choice that caused the effect
We refuse to accept that we are the fallen of God's best

If we're His best, can you imagine the worst
We who claim to have the answers
We fall at the drop of a dime
There is no staying power to those who profess it loudest

The Body of Christ, a rebellious army
Without the unity, we will fall without remedy
It's no one else's fault anymore
It's time we accept it
We are the fallen of God's best

Confusion

Lost in a storm cloud of emotions
Thought I was in love
But was only going through the motions

Said I was happy, but really was not
Now I'm over him, but still miss him a lot

Lost what I wanted to find what I had
Learned how to be happy when I was really sad
But of all things, I learned to wait
As long as I live, it is never too late

Never too late for me to live again
Nor purge my life from ungodly men
Never too late to make amends
Never too late to change my friends

He hurt me and used me so that it scarred me deep
But I know it was only my harvest to reap
Now is the time to stop the pain
Now is the time to live again
Now that I have learned from my mistake
I'll do what I must for Christ's sake

Questions of Him

What can you say
To tell him how you feel
Will he ever know
Everything you said was real

Where can you go
To escape your past mistake
Where can you run to
Which direction can you take

When he knows your faults
Can he still meet your need
When he can see your downfalls
Will he still want to lead

When he can tell you love him
But doesn't know how much
Will he take advantage of you
Turn your love into a crutch

Do you really want him to know
Tell him about what's inside
Do you trust him to understand
Or will he take you for a ride

Trapped Between Two

In my first months of salvation

Here I go again
Trapped between two
Which will win
What is the right thing to do

Following God is what I desire
But who can quench this world's fire
I love the Lord with all my heart
But worldly cares are tearing me apart

One day I'm up
The next I'm down
One day I'm lost
The next I'm found

God, I choose to do what's right
And now that I do
Show me how to live in the light
That I may walk with you

Shades of Red

Sizzling hot, boiling romance
The ways of passion inside
Dreamy eyes
Soft hands
Taking me for a ride

Saved the same, loved the best
The favor of God resides
Preach alike
Worship the same
Dedication to God that won't die

He's everything, all wrapped up
A leader, a lover, a real man
Firm instructions
Gentle guidance
No reason to date again

Shades of red, the spring is here
This man I want to know
Passion and promise
Kindness and truth
Let's see where this thing will go

My Husband, Your Wife

Lost then found
Hide then seek
Everything has an order
Pride before meek

And so it is with us, me and you
How often must I pour out my heart to you

It was just me
Along you came
Together just us two
But with your baggage it wasn't the same

My husband, your wife
Your plans
My life
To find togetherness in division

Wanting you beside me in every decision
My husband, your wife
Our plans
Our life

Watching and Wondering

Watching as he walks away
Wondering how he feels
Wishing I hadn't waken up today
Waiting to know if all this is real

How can he just forget me
How can he leave me now
Has he fallen out of love with me
If I can have him back, tell me how

It hurts to be tossed aside
And left out in the cold
It crushes all your pride
Makes you feel useless and old

How I wish for the days gone by
When he belonged to me
I think about it with a sigh
Some things aren't meant to be

Yet I'm watching as he walks away
Wondering how he feels
I wish I hadn't waken up today
Maybe none of this is real

The Rain

The drops of rain run down my face
But yet the sun does shine
Hoping the water washes away the trace
Of a love that was once mine

The tears mix with the rain
To hide what I really feel
To wash my soul of the pain
To show me this love was real

It seems the rain does come on time
To catch the emotions of life
As if life has an eternal rhyme
Like a surgeon with a knife

God designed nature in such an awesome way
Able to change how we feel on any given day
The rain can make you feel soft and gentle
Able to make you sentimental

Yet it can raise up turbulent emotions
Or it can work as a love potion
The rain may fall gentle or violent
The rain tells a story, though it's silent!

His Name Is Jesus

What happens when focus is lost
When decisions are made, who pays the cost
Who has to lose for another to win
God can't you see the shape we are in

How can praise help when you're going through
Is anyone willing to be there for you
Is there someone willing to pay the price
Who on earth can give some good advice

I know a man who lived long ago
Though He was a king, He lived pretty low
Though He had much power, He was kind
I didn't see Him, but He was a friend of mine

His name is Jesus, the great Immanuel
The great "I Am" who never fails
He gave his life for all my woes
He went to hell to conquer my foes

He sees the shape we are in
But He says be still, you are free from sin
He says just trust and obey
And let the Lord have His way

Rollers in My Hair

All the people begin to stare
Wonder what they are looking at
Walking past them in a stupor
Not realizing the object of their attention

Trying to catch a glimpse of myself
I look to the left in the window
Frightened by the sight staring back at me
There are rollers in my hair

My God, what was I thinking
Must one always remember the hair
The beautifying, mystifying hair
The hair that feels like silk to touch

More people are staring
Looking at what must be a spectacle
I walk past them with my stupor gone
I have rollers in my hair

Schism in the Body

My heart and my head don't agree
My head knows things my heart can't see
My heart desires the love it recently lost
My head doesn't want to pay the cost

My heart aches for him at night when I'm alone
My head says it's too late, he's already gone
My spirit keeps praying to God for relief
But my heart has to come to that belief

God is more powerful than what I feel
He can deliver me, it's just another ordeal
I lay awake at night and can't sleep
Because my feelings run so deep

My love, it's hard to be without you
But that's what I have to do
I'm not ashamed of losing this man
There is one for me in God's plan

So heart and head, let's just agree
That the Spirit knows what's best for me

It Hurts

Like a child that bumps his knee
This wonderful man ran to me
In the heat of the night
And far out of sight
It was him I began to know
As our feelings began to grow
It's him that I cherish and hold so dear
And him who I want to keep near
But being tossed aside brings doubt
Questions of what the relationship was about
Trying really hard, but failing really bad
What made me happy now makes me sad
It hurts to think I trusted in vain
For him to turn away while I'm in pain
Crying for hours with no relief
Feeling like the victim of a thief
What can mend a broken heart
When the love you had is torn apart
It hurts to see the end of a good thing
To realize it was nothing more than a fling
Oh, it hurts to be rejected and refused
To find that your love has been abused
But it only made me fall on my face
To take inventory and change my pace
To seek my God, Comforter and Friend
So my broken heart he can mend
Yes, I'm hurt but I'll make it through
It's all that's left for me to do

Cover Me

If in my life you find a fault
Or something I do causes an alt
Cover me

If it seems that I'm always sick
And my temper flares too quick
If when you speak to me, I turn my head
And you find a man in my bed
Cover me

If I don't smile throughout the day
And if my attitude gets in the way
If you see me overtaken in sin
Without your prayers, I won't win
Please cover me

Lift me up in prayer and lay on your face
Beseech the Lord to wrap me in grace
Seek Him for my strength so that I can stand
That I will never let go of His hand
Ask Him to have mercy on me
To open my eyes so that I will see
All I ask is that you cover me

If We Had Thought

Who would have thought
It would be me and you
Who would have thought
One day I would hold you

Did you ever think
You could love one like me
Did you ever think
You'd desire something that couldn't be

I never thought
Love could hurt so bad
I never thought
Missing you would make me this sad

Nobody thought
We had a chance
Nobody thought
We had a true romance

We should have thought
What is God's will
If we had thought
We would be together still

The Salvation of a Mary

I know the pains, have felt the strain
Of trying to be in love
But in all I do, I try to be true
To my self and my God above

Women suffer emotional hell
Giving themselves to a guy
So often relationships fail
And we're left wondering why

The woes, the sorrows, like no tomorrow
Can drain away your life
Bedding man after man, with no real plan
Adding only to the strife

Sex is not the answer to anything you feel
It's simply another problem, another ordeal
Only God can heal you, give you self-worth
Only God is able to give you a new birth

Hard life led you to internal divisions
But godly life leads to better decisions
Let go of your past, my child, be healed
With our Jesus, your fate is sealed!

Tired of Being Judged

I find that my worth in the eyes of others
Is worth very little
No matter what I do in this walk
My testimony seems yet brittle
People talk all day long
Judging what I wear
Everything is immoral
Even my hair
If I defend myself, then I'm wrong
They tell me just be quiet
If I obey and take it silently
Most of them still don't buy it
I'm so tired of being judged
And taken for granted
"She'll never change, she'll never change!"
Is all they've ever chanted
For the day I was born
Up until now
Everyone has an opinion
I need to escape somehow
Even my destiny
Sometimes I want to forfeit it
I cry out to God
But He just says forget it
Though I'm tired, I'm not through
Though sometimes I'm weary, God is always true

Samuel

So much love shared between us
How can one deny
So many days of commitment
A dedication that will not die
A storm came through our lives
It shook the ground on which we stand
But the sun had to shine
Our love began to grow again
Samuel, my judge, my prophet, my priest
Samuel, my man, my friend, my release

No one can change who you are in God
Though so many of them try
Let them talk and laugh at you
But never let them see you cry
I am here by your side
Never will I depart
I will lift you up
Because you are the beat of my heart
Samuel, my judge, my prophet, my priest
Samuel, my man, my friend, my release

In Place of the Husband

When I was down
He held on to me
When I cried
He comforted me

Standing in as the tangible arms
He takes my fears away
Advocating my Savior
He provides a safe place for me to stay

How can this man be the one
He was found in an unlikely place
There was nothing attractive about him
No sign saying special on his face

Kind of like my Lord
He seems to always be around
Rooted in commitment
There is much love to be found

In the place of my husband
There stands a friend
He will always be just that
At least that until the end

Exotic Details

The way you look at me makes me melt
The most sensual thing I've ever felt
Imagining your voice in my ear
Just like yesterday, I can still hear
Your bass whispering to me
Telling me you're in love with me

Each time I sleep, I dream of you
And all the things we're yet to do
Every time I hear your name
I blush publicly without any shame

I remember the first time you touched me
A forehead kiss, as gentle as can be
I remember every phone call
And every encounter, big or small

Exotic details of a relationship gone
Leaving me to feel so alone
Still I have my dreams of you
I guess they will have to do
If ever a chance is given to me
I would make things like they used to be

The Scorpion's Aries

Let me tell you about my two Aries
That filled my life with uncertainties

The first was to me a dream by day
You know the kind that evaporates away
Those three months brought me three years of pain
I felt so close to going insane

The second was like a cruise on open seas
His smile was like a gentle breeze
His eyes were like the rays of the sun
And I still love him second to none

But loving an Aries for a Scorpio
Is like talking back to a radio
They don't forgive and are easily hurt
Just their mean look can make you feel like dirt

Yet I loved them both and love them still
Even sometimes against my will
If I've learned anything from these two men
It's that I'll never date an Aries again

The Debate

There is no way to get back all that was lost
And what was taken came at a high cost
Now as I try to put the pieces back together
I must first find out rather
What I had is really what I need
Do I just let go of the treacherous deed
That was done to me at a young age
Or do I simply turn the page

Can I forgive those who once used me
And let them off scott-free
Or do I want to hold this grudge
That fills my heart with dark sludge
Shouldn't I try to make them pay
For what was done to me on that day
Is it wrong for me to want them sad
Because their deed hurt me so bad

I don't know how to feel
I want to shout, kick or kill
But God said, "Vengeance is mine"
And to me that's just fine

The Patter of Little Feet

Little eyes
Little feet
Little hands
All over me

What a dream, to have a child
To awaken to late night cries
How could something so natural
Be so hard to obtain

It was said I was a woman
But might as well be a man
Everywhere I go there are those little people
I feel stuck, waiting on a miracle
Understanding why they call it a miracle
They are so hard to come by

Waiting to hear the patter of little feet
But how long, O Lord, must I wait
You know this is my dream
Come now Jesus and heal me
Make my body whole
So I can hear the patter of little feet

Mama's Little Boy

There is no one like mama's little boy
When he smiles it brings me such joy
He is a gift to me, appreciated indeed
He was given to me when I was most in need

The only little one from my womb to live
The only little one God has chosen to give
Yet, I thank Him for this child
With praises for a decade, that would be mild

So many have a barren womb
And in their hearts is only a tomb
Burying the dream of having a baby
Yet somehow they hold on to maybe

Maybe one day I will have a girl or boy
Who will indeed bring me joy
But those dreams go unfulfilled
And all those hopes are eventually killed

That is why I'm grateful for the one I got
There are too many that have not

Solondra

Solondra, my daughter, my little girl
My dream, my desire, my whole world

How long did I pray
Wanting you, my twin
How long did I wait
But a princess I did win

God surprised me with you
You came at a time when I was blue
But you brightened my day
You made me smile
Each time you kicked
It hurt for a while

I went in labor
Oh, the pain and the grief
Had my daughter
What a relief

I love you so much
The joy of my heart
Wouldn't trade you for the world
Of me you are a part

The Preacher

Who is the preacher
Is he simply a teacher
Why all the shouts
Is it to destroy the doubts

When do they take a breath
Is it only after death
Does he ever cry
Does he ask God why

Does he ever feel alone
When all his followers are gone
Will he let himself go
Or will he allow himself to grow

Does he really believe
In the Word he receive
Or does he preach a lie
Allowing his life to go by

All through the night
This is his fight
Yet, with the passing of days
With the Lord he stays

Act 4

Restoration and Destiny

Not Consumed, Just Burned

I wasn't consumed, I was just burned
I didn't just hear, but this time I learned
There is a God who watches over me
All my wrongs He can see

All my time He controls
So I've learned to let go
I've learned to lean and depend on Him
I've learned to trust and wait on Him

I've learned in Him I can confide
And there is nothing from Him I can hide
It's like being bear on the highest mount
In front of the One I must give an account

A consuming fire, my God, my Judge
Able to forgive, never holding a grudge
Yet this time, I wasn't consumed but burned
I guess I'll call it a lesson learned

Faithful Lover

How good it must be for your lover to return
How wonderful and excellent is his love
So long has it stood the test of time
Through so many storms and rain

The infidelity, the lies
Deceit and distrust
Yet it stood through the trials
Never did he stray

Never did he leave
He was there all the time, waiting on me
Then at the night of our reunion
He held me closely once again

Reminding me of true love
Causing my heart to melt
The remembrance of our intimacy
Brings back the love I once had

To taste it again
Allows me to know
Never will I stray again
From God, my faithful lover

Valleys

Valleys can be a wonderful place
No one sees you there
Your name has no face to it
No matter what you go through, it's you

Valleys are private places
Though you're lonely, you're never alone
The valley is the place of purging
The valley is the place of self-recognition

Oh, my valley experiences
They have shown my true self to me
The little, troubled me
The deeply, remorseful me

The lonely me
And the beautiful me
Oh God, you alone know my valley
And you alone know me

Valleys of life are to be expected
Valleys, my low points
How much have I learned from the valley
Now I journey to the mountain

My Father

Once upon a time I had a goal
Until pain scarred my soul
Then someone taught me how to pray
Since then I do it everyday

But when I'm seen talking to God
People seem to think I'm a bit odd
They don't know about His saving grace
Or how I got to this place

They were not there when He spared me
Many are blind and cannot see
But I could tell the story of suicide
How through my own hands I could have died

How through my weakness, God made me strong
I was set free by being done wrong
Though I've suffered, I'm still here
With God keeping me from my biggest fear

I've been in a long lasting storm
But God made sure I stayed warm
Then He brought me out with a mighty hand
And set my feet on dry land

The good news I'm determined to share
Because my Father really does care

No More Fear

With trembling and fear
I draw near
But that isn't how you want me
You hold me dear
Now it is clear
That's not how it should be

With you is true love
You are the one God above
You are who we need
You take the lead

Allow your children to know
About a broken reed
Who was your seed
The first born you did sow

God, I do love you
It has been tried and is true
To you I give my existence
No matter what I do
I will always serve you
Never to give you resistance

The Flow of Water

Water flows from the center of love
The center of a sacrifice
Water cleans and purifies my soul
My mind, my desire, my emotions

Look at the fleeting day
Running away from truth
But can never escape water
Water that runs the distance

The distance of my pain
The distance of my distress
Bringing forth my joy
In moments of the storm

In the eye of the storm
I see the water
How it flows so softly
Yet how powerful must it be

It washed away my sin
Made me ready for that great day
Water flows from the center of love
The center of a dead Savior

Ways of Passion

Who can understand the ways of passion
It seems to consume a man
It takes his thoughts well beyond ration
And makes him go against his own plan

He seems to forget about consequences
Taking a gamble with chance
Not considering hostile incidences
And with his destiny does he dance

Desire kills all his dreams
And topples all his wealth
Nothing is what it seems
His heart has lost its health

His mind is filled with thoughts of her
A woman well out of reach
Wondering how he might possess her
If she is the kind he can teach

Oh, man of God, flee youthful lusts
Rebuke them at the start
To live godly, it's a must
And let God do the other part

To Satisfy You

It is my desire to be in your Will
And for your kingdom to be filled with zeal
To behave myself as part of your flock
To stand on you because you are the rock

To stand in faith without any fear
For you to always have my ear
I am a branch of your True Vine
From me your light will always shine

Into the darkness it will permeate
Leading people into the straight gate
I want people to always see
You are the greatest part of me

To satisfy you, I will pay any cost
Not one second of my life will be lost
I will spend it being obedient
Doing only the things that are expedient

The Great I AM, my El Shaddai
You don't expect me to be perfect, just that I try
And try I will all the days of my existence
The key to please you is persistence

Here I Am

Here I am, if you're looking for me
Standing here, plain to see
Waiting on you to make a choice
Waiting for you to heed my voice

Waiting on you to decide to live
Waiting to show what I have to give
Here I am, right beside you
Here I am, sending out blessings to you

Loving and leading
Touching and pleading
Looking and listening
Paying close attention

Waiting on the day you need me
Waiting for you to bow down to me
To acknowledge all my splendor
Waiting for you to surrender

So I can stretch out my arm to thee
Here I am, if you're looking for me

Sinner and Saint

Broken and torn
Rent and worn
But in all the pain I found something great
For all the troubles, I learned to wait

My God is faithful and just to forgive
A peaceful life He wants me to live
But peace is only found after a storm
Cold must come before you enjoy being warm

Trouble burns away selfish care
Turmoil on the inside teaches us to share
Pain of the heart draws us away from wrong
But after some suffering, we have a new song

We can sing of the joy after all is done
We can celebrate the death of the Son
The only difference between sinner and saint
Is one can make it through, the other can't

Warfare

What can you say
When tragedy comes your way
What do you do
When attacks are aimed at you
How can you fight what you cannot see
These are the questions roiling around in me
More than myself, I love my son
The enemy has to pay for what he's done
I'm out for blood, sweat and tears
For restoration of our stolen years
In my inconvenience, all I desire
Is to bring this thing down to the wire
To free my son from the bondage inside
And introduce him to his Savior that died
So that what the devil meant for bad
He can let it be good
So that even while he's sad
He will do what he should
Offense comes, but we have a choice
We can react or we can rejoice
For me, the attack renewed my zeal
Though we can't see him, the devil is real
He hates us and wants us to pay
For what will come to him on judgment day
Now my job is to witness even more
Not to be grounded, but to really soar
To show my child how to break free
And be all God has chosen him to be
I'm determined to make God's presence known
Until what time the kingdom is full grown

Toss It Out

When the salad goes bad in the fridge
You need to toss it out
When a bad apple spoils the bunch
You need to toss them out
When your friends encourage you to do wrong
Please toss them out

There are some things not good for us
And it has to be put away
There are some things that will destroy us
If we keep it even one more day

When we come to a place where something smells
Whatever it is must go
No matter what affects your life negatively
This is something you should know

Don't be afraid to toss things out
Not everything is for you to keep
Some things were only temporary
To hold them will make you weep

When fish begins to smell in your fridge
You need to toss it out
When poached eggs decide to rot
You need to toss them out
Whatever you find that's too much of a burden
Don't be afraid to toss it out

Some things must go and this you need to know

Oxymoron

Once in a while
You may find
Something wonderful
That blows your mind

It's always been there
Right in your face
In the most unlikely place

Sometimes life will toss you in the worst direction
Only that you may find true protection
You don't know good until you experience bad
To be truly happy, you must first be sad

You can't understand free until you've been bound
Until you can't hear, you won't appreciate sound
All the best things that I couldn't see
Appeared the worst things at that time to me

Who's to Say

What does life hold for me
When you take a look
What do you see

A woman of beauty, one that is kind
Or a woman of destiny
One with Christ on her mind

Can you see the path I'm on
Or do you see a dream
Can you look at me and tell what's wrong
Or only how it seems

Who's to say what's to come
Or what life holds in store
I know that God is my source
And life only promises me more

More time, more joy, more peace
A love that will never cease

Love for My Savior

As I sit and think of what to say
My heart takes a minute to pray
I love you more than words can express
Though so much of it I often repress

I can't contain the joy when I hear your name
I jump and shout without any shame
When you touch me I tingle inside
What I feel for you supersedes pride

I find myself being desperate for you
There is no one who can replace you
I wake up early to seek your face
I lie down late in your embrace

You are to me the total sum
More than my past and what shall come
In your face I find that I am whole
Just to be in your presence soothes my soul

And at the end of my life, one thing I know
Where you are I will be there also

Solomon's Appeal

What do you know about Solomon's song
Can you tell me how the appeal lasted so long
Is it because love is a lifelong walk
Or is all that romance just senseless talk

Rise my love, come away with me
In your arms, I've been made free
You are so beautiful, the apple of my eye
I only want to lift you up high

Holding on tight, never letting go
Causing this love to continually grow
Consuming passion, kisses sweet as a berry
A romantic love that makes the heart merry

Solomon, the excellence of your name
Alighting in me an eternal flame
I am your sister, spouse and friend
We have devotion that will never end

My compassion stirs for you
You are the beginning of everything true
Majesty, lover, eternal King
Of your great affection I will sing

Fairest among thousands, my chosen one
Altogether lovely, God's Son
I've set you as a seal upon my heart
So that from you I will never depart

Act 5

Love Found Me?

Conflict

The beauty of a new day
The fear of facing it
The prospects of a new way
The fear of taking it

The joy of a new man
The fear of being used
The time to take a new stand
The remembrance of being abused

Conflict, Conflict
And confusion everywhere
See a land beyond the hills
No directions to get there

Then comes Jesus, my guide and friend
Here comes Jesus to step right in
But what of those who have Him
But cannot hear His voice
What of those who love Him
But continually make the wrong choice

And yet there remains a new day
But the fear of facing it

Orchids and Lilies

In the middle of spring
New love begins
When the trees give blossom
Old love ends

As roses give off a great aroma
I stand in the fields of my mind
As the breeze carries sweet smells of love
Its owner I desire to find

Never will this spring end in our hearts
It was the time we began to dance
As orchids and lilies envelope each other
We welcome a lovely romance

As you look longingly upon me
I find solace in your eyes
Even when confusion finds me
I take comfort knowing you are wise

You are my love, my wonder and my man
You bring me joy and help me to understand
You can do most anything you choose
And your love is too great for me to lose

Orchids are the commitment between me and you
Lilies are the love shared between us two

The Man

As the sun rises, life centers in on me
Falling in love, how can it be
He was a dream, a whisper at midnight
He is the sun, shining ever so bright

At a time like this, here he is
Deep in my heart, I am his
Looking, longing, waiting for a touch
It's all about this man I love so much
I find myself daring to believe
I'm in a place where I can receive

His love is sweet, opening my eyes to see
That being in love makes me free
He holds me and washes away my tears
Late into the night, he kisses away my fears

Can a life that started wrong
End with such a wonderful song
I belong to him, and more than I can say
It's his love that gets me through the day
This man, my love, the stars in my sky
This man who keeps me lifted up so high

The Connection

The favor of God is upon my life
Receiving my husband
Becoming his wife
The two of us meet
We instantly agree
This love connection is meant to be

Our eyes locked
Our hearts began to flutter
Could barely murmur a word
All I could do was stutter

The relationship began to grow
Everyday we prayed
We talked often on the phone
For hours and hours we stayed

Never could replace you
Never would I try
Will always love you
Until the day we die

Great is your love, your kiss, your touch
This relationship means so very much

The Scorpions Meet

Can two that are alike in so many ways
Come together for the rest of their days
Can they put their similarities aside
And let go of all their pride
Can these two trust each other
To be there for one another

Two Scorpions meet together
To determine whether
What they have is worth the fight

These two people, loyal indeed
Able to meet each other's needs
In bed and out
These two know what it's all about
These two people may be meant to be
It's apparent for all to see

Two Scorpions meet together
Just to determine whether
What they have is worth the fight

Trust Him, dear Scorpions, and only believe
Even you two can receive
God is able to make it turn out alright
All you have to do is pray and fight

Charmed

Dear Sir, your charisma becomes you
And so does your voice
But even your smile betrays you
And speaks of your choice

There's a twinkle in your eyes
And a warm look on your face
To my great surprise
You have taken up a space

Now you reside in my heart
Branding your symbol there
Our friendship is only the start
Of us, the perfect pair

You, my prince, have my heart alarmed
Your very essence has permeated my soul
Your passion has me charmed
To make you love me is my goal

Love Is...

Love is walks in the park
Love is holding hands in the dark
Love is soothing, sweet and kind
Love is having a peace of mind

Love is understanding that special someone
Love is gazing at the moon and sun
Love is honest and always true
Love is what connects me to you

Love is what makes my heart beat fast
Love is our present, future and past
Love is the gentleness in your voice
Love is had only by choice

Love is your touch, your laugh and your smile
Love is the essence of your style
Love is a slow fall off the cliff of thought
Love is the jewel most often sought

Come my love, dive with me
Into the abyss of love just over this sea
Come my prize, my treasured one
Love is to be had in the Son

Real Man

Valor in a man
It's God's plan
And oh, how beautiful to be found
In this land
There's none that understand
Few men of integrity around

Men that fight
For what's right
Men that woo your very heart
Men with might
That walk in the light
Men honest from the start

Men who love and who have lost
Men willing to pay the cost
Men who will not cheat or leave
And to their wife they will cleave

Those who love God and His way
Who love you all night
And work for you all day
A REAL man!!!

In Love

The man behind the mask
Who is he
The man under the suit
Who is he

I love the man with the mask
But will I love him without it
I love the man with the suit
There's no doubt about it

Can you love something you know not
Or is that just a dream
Can a person stay in love
When things aren't what they seem

Oh, God, my father, help me out
Line me up on a new route
God, I love him
That's all I know
Can't get enough of him
And with him I will grow

Love has found me
And in love I will be

Love Defined

There are never any words to truly express
I try all the more, but succeed all the less
This enigma, the undefined
This great mystery that can't be confined
This little word has survived throughout the ages
Found in many books on countless pages
This tiny word that conquerors great men
And when misplaced leads to sin
Such a small word with great implications
Causing wars and dividing nations
But in it's finest, oh how grand
Easily felt, but hard to understand
It came from a place far away
And grows more each passing day
Frequently said, but never enough
Often surrounded by other stuff
Lifting the spirit while tickling the ear
This word is still held most dear
Husbands, wives and mothers
Children, friends and brothers
The comfort this word can often bring
Setting us free, letting the praises ring
Love, that splendid and sensational thought
Love, the desire most often sought
Love, a marvelous word indeed
Love, not a desire, but a need

The Man in My Life

There is this man whom I love
Sent as his help from above
There when I cry, there when I call
There when I'm up, there when I fall

He is a gift, sent in disguise
Hidden from the foolish, revealed to the wise
Though he fumbles at holding my hand
I recognize that he is still my man

Though not perfect, he is really sweet
There are few able to fill his seat
He's not gorgeous, but enough for me
To my heart, he holds the key

To this man, I must say
Though I yell, I love you anyway
I appreciate you being here
To my heart, you are dear

I'm not the easiest boat to sail
But with God, we won't fail
I thank you God for the man in my life
It's truly a blessing to be his wife

His Light

Sunshine, rain
Love and pain
Joy in my sorrow
Hope for tomorrow

There's a chance
For love and romance
In every life around
At first glance
We decided to dance
And true love was what we found

His salvation and mine
He's powerful, I'm kind
But we have joy in our home
In his love will I dine
Every mistake is fine
There is no reason for me to roam

God keeps him, He keeps me
From moving beyond what's right
On wedding night it's as it should be
We lay together in His light

Man for Me

Him who knows God
Him who loves God
Him who will sacrifice for God
Him who will worship God
He is the one I need

One who can teach me
One who can love me
One who can understand me
One who can protect me
This one is the one I want

He will pray to God
He will serve God
He will praise God
He will obey God
He is the husband for me

This man will guide me
This man will hold me
This man will comfort me
This man will challenge me
This is the man for me

Love for You

Love is something often confused
If it's not taken care of
It is often abused

Love knows no color and sees no bounds
When you stop looking
It will often be found

Love is dedicated and always true
It comes into your life
It changes you

Real love never dies
It lives through thick and thin
Even when it makes you cry
It keeps you free from sin

There's this one I love so much
And when he's not around
I miss his touch

So long now
This love is real
It has been tested
It's still what I feel

Yep, You're In Love

Cheerful looks, glittering eyes
The glow of love on your face
Sly grins, delightful cries
Pleasure no one can erase

Though some may try
They give up with a sigh
For love pleads its own case
Nights of yes, nights of no
But the bond remains strong
Days of joy, days of woe
But can still admit when you're wrong

You know you're in love
When the skies above
Seem to sing to you a personal song
It's as if God himself is there
And really He is
Teaching you how to share
And how great love is

When love is what you have found
There is nothing more precious around

God, I Love Rick James

Moonlight shines upon the face of my love
It causes the water to glisten
His face is radiant, full of joy
His body glowing in the dawn of our love
God gave him ebony eyes

Beautiful brown eyes pierce my soul
Awakening a slumbering love
Necking and loving in the wake of day
Up all night reveling in his warmth
God gave him ebony eyes

He prayed for me
Then he touched my cheek
He kissed my face
Whispering sweet nothings in my ear
God gave him ebony eyes

God let me love him forever
Only to be surpassed by my love for You!

He Was There

His hands reach for mine
I feel a slight squeeze
As I lie there in pain
I hear him begin to pray

As the sun begins to shine upon my bed
I notice him crying
He holds my hand tightly
As his other hand strokes my head

Soon the pain begins to subside
I realize the jewel of my sickness
I found a true companionship in my man
He was there the whole time

Now we lie together in bed
I thank God for the gift of my husband
I caress him for all those sleepless nights
All the times he held my hand
And I love him in the sight of God

Rumor of Love

I heard a rumor once upon a time
Long ago, before love was mine

Seems to be
Love is hard to find
Some tell me
It puts you in a bind

But that's not the case
Not with the love I found
I wasn't looking
But love was around

Some often say, love is easy to run away
Maybe none know love's name
Real love is God
He's always the same

Now I've found another
This man in my life
It won't be long
I'll be his wife

A Touch

Love was the word we said
Passion was the dance we done
Romance was the song we sang
Desire was the game we played
Until it all backfired in our face

Hatred took the place of love
Coldness overshadowed our passion
Boredom set in and ran romance away
Repulsive thoughts we had for each other
Until a lady came into our lives

Jesus was the name she called
God was the ruler of all
The Spirit was the peace she gave
The Word was the guidance she used
Now once again we have found one another

How can things get so bad, and then...
One touch from the Lord makes us glad

In My Sickness

Waking up in pain, achy and alone
I find myself calling you on the phone
Desiring your presence in my time of need
As my body grows your seed

In my sickness, I find a reprieve
Your ceaseless prayers make me believe
That in my weaknesses, I can lean on you
You will be here no matter what I do

In my sickness, I realize how you care
Ardent affection is in the air
You hold my hand through my tears
Promising to be there over the years

In my sickness, I've fallen deeper
Realizing the more, you are a keeper
You've proven your love for me
And shown me things that will be

I want to say thank you and I appreciate
All you've done, small and great

Surprised

It seems the sun shines in the most unlikely place
When you feel lost, it hits you in the face
How it was with us, a big surprise
When we weren't looking, love began to rise

No one can now make it cease
With each passing day, it seems to increase
I would have never guessed from the day we met
That you and I would become a perfect set

Now that you have become more than a friend
I don't want this relationship to ever end
I want to be your woman and become your wife
You are who with I want to share my life

I want you to know I'm dedicated to you
And I promise to always be true
If my life takes me around the world
I will always be your girl

There may be times when you make me mad
Or something you say makes me sad
But it won't change how much I care
I promise to always be there

Until the time death makes us part
Even then you will die with my heart

YOU

A relationship requires so much more
Than giving a kiss as you walk through the door
So many women go unfulfilled each day
And we have no idea how to say
We are in need of more from you
Not just what you say, but what you do

We try each day to look good for you
And to our vows we stay true
We wear uncomfortable things for your ego
And when you want our bodies, we don't say no
We cook and clean and have your babies
But all we get in return are ifs, buts and maybes

We want nights out at the movie-plex
We want to be held without having sex
We want you to hear us when we speak
And to be compassionate when we feel weak
We not only want your body, but also your mind
And for you to stop pretending to be blind
To the things going on around you
And take responsibility for what you do

We want you to miss us while we're gone
And to stop being so quick to leave us alone
We love you guys through the good and bad
Even if you take us for granted or make us mad
Surely, some man will listen and take heed
And give us what we truly need...
YOU!

Act 6

The Long Exhale

Anticipation

I hear the whispers of your name late into the night
Holding to your voice, I try to bring you into sight
But no matter how I try, I can't bring you near
As much as I want to, I can't get you here

My heart continues to ache
Longing for your touch
Night after night, I can only dream
Because I miss you so much

I reason in myself
Soon you will be free
And for the rest of my life
You will be with me

Oh, love of my life
When will you return
There's so much about you
And so much I've yet to learn

All I have right now are memories
Still, those I appreciate
But one day soon, I'll have you
You will be my mate

Make Me Pretty

The effects of warfare show in my face
Is there something that will erase
All the scars left on me
So that others cannot see
All the mistakes I try to hide away
And the battles I lost along the way

I do understand it was for a reason
That my life often had warring seasons
The lashes, the bruises and all I've been through
Has affected how I see and all I do
My countenance suffers from what people said
But I know you are the lifter of my head

The cry of my heart is make me pretty

Make me a delight in a land of shame
Allow my hardships to glorify your name
Take the yoke of bondage off my neck
Repair me from my train wreck
Beautify my spirit and dear Lord, please heal
Keep me in the midst of your perfect will

The cry of my heart is make me pretty

Pretty to me is being centered in you
Being unafraid to rest in you
Pretty to me is looking like you
Doing only the things you would have me to do

Hold Up My Arms

Sometimes living gets the best of me
I lose my focus and become unable to see
I've been tainted by all the trials
I've grown weak over all the miles

Hold up my arms when I tire
Don't let my strength completely expire

Sometimes I've taken wrong turns
Had situations that left burns
Sometimes I've cried all night long
Wondering where I went wrong
At times I've lost my desire to fight
Wanted to give up doing what was right
Some nights I wrestled to the break of day
Trying to make my troubles go away

Hold up my arms when I tire
Don't let my strength completely expire

If I don't have support from you
What else am I supposed to do
Who else can I count, who will take heed
I'm trying to say it's you I need
Please, hold up my arms when I tire
Don't let my strength completely expire
Don't give the enemy an edge over me
Whether you do or do not agree
I need you

Still Waters Run Deep

I've looked upon many waters
And seen the flow of tears
I've noticed the blending of them
All through the years

This leads me on a journey
What are the issues of my heart
What kind of waters run inside me
Where should my faith trek start

Is my love like a deep ocean
Will the surface fool you
Or is my love like a stream
Running right past you

Is my devotion like a river
Or is it like a pond
Will it change with the seasons
Or does it create a permanent bond

Still waters run deep
With love, the deeper they go
Sometimes they are lost inside us
When our life is filled with woe

Still waters run so deep
They are entangled in our being
But at the time when they are released
Still waters can be freeing

What a Sacrifice

Though I'm here now, you don't know my sacrifice
Since you didn't live it with me
My testimony must suffice

There were times when I didn't sleep all night
And all day long I prayed
Couldn't discern which way was right
And on my knees I stayed

I've been tested on what I say
And have given up many things
I've quite often gone the wrong way
And lost the joy obedience brings
I've endured ridicule and shame
Finding no way out
Often knowing I was to blame
Walking in so much doubt

It was a sacrifice to change my manner
The metamorphosis was so extensive
But through it all, God was my banner
And the love He gave me was intensive
The cover won't tell what's in the book
You must look once more
Don't ever judge things by how they look
Go deeper, down to the very core

Though I'm here now, you don't know my sacrifice
Since you didn't live it with me
My testimony must suffice

A Desire to Praise

Each day that passes, I find a new reason
And with every passing season
There is a desire to praise

In my times of deepest sorrow
He gave me hope for tomorrow
With all the promises He has made to me
It should be easy for you to see
I have a desire to praise

All my situations are working for the good
All things end as they should
No matter what the enemy throws my way
God is my protection, both night and day
I have a desire to praise

As I lift up my head and use my voice
I realize praise isn't a feeling but a choice
It's my decision to extol His name
To continuously spread His fame
I have a desire to praise

Though sometimes I don't want to utter a thing
I realize the joys praise will bring
It's a weapon for me when I'm down
It's an anchor for me so I won't drown
In the worst of darkness, praise is a light
Helping me to regain my sight
I have a desire to praise

The Legacy

A warm smile
A friendly word
Books of encouragement
Children full of the Word
What will I leave behind

Small gestures of love
A hug, a kiss, an embrace
Small proofs of my existence
Pictures, tapes, everything in it's place
What will I leave behind

Fortunes of wisdom and knowledge
Gained over the years
Tidbits of information
I've collected from my peers
What else might I leave behind

Will I leave memories
Painful to bear
Will I leave a trail of tears
Or a cloak of debt to wear
What will you leave behind

Healing Poetry

Poetry is therapeutic because it's real
The more you write, the more you heal
It comes out of you from deep inside
Where pain and pleasure, as a couple, abide

My mother used to let her words flow
The burdens would lift and she'd begin to glow
I knew then poetry is a treasure
One too great for us to measure

It seemed so easy for her to do
Of course, back then I didn't have a clue
Poetry is the counselor of the almost insane
The best of it is birthed out of pain

Some of the verses that move us to tears
Came from the poet's best and worst years
How can they be both at the same time
Because the life of a poet is like the life of a mime

The more pain he feels, the better he seems to be
What's right before your eyes, you can't see
So we hide in plain sight
What you call our greatest day
Is really our most agonizing night

Poetry is therapeutic because it's real
What you read is what we feel

Explicitly

Thoughts of you come frequently
Leaving me panting and wanting more
Often I envision you
Then my spirit seems to soar

Explicitly desiring what is already mine
You bring light to my life and make me to shine

Your love is described as extravagant
Excessively poured upon me
Oh, how I yearn the more for it
Its power makes me free

Explicitly desiring what is already mine
You bring light to my life and make me to shine

My nakedness doesn't bother you
To you, it's as the break of day
With your eyes you've seen it all
And still you choose to stay

Explicitly desiring what is already mine
Because you're so good to me, I am forever thine

Heaven, a Beautiful Place

Leisure of the mind
Pleasure of the body
Joy in the heart
A smile on the face
Heaven must be a beautiful place

Foods of all kinds
Desserts as far as the eye can see
Drinks that quench the thirst
And the man of all men right beside me
Heaven is the place I want to be

Togetherness and love
Singing songs of merriment
Humming tunes of satisfaction
Whistling with the birds
Heaven has to be more than words
Heaven is my home
Though my journey has prolonged my return
Heaven is the final destination
Where I can experience true elation

Act 7

The Ceremony

A Desired Love

Of all the things for which I desire and care
There is one I want to share
It's called love, the simple kind
The variety not so easy to find
The love of a man, to rest in his arms
One who will woo me with his charms
A love that's faithful, sweet and true
To rest on my heart like morning dew
A gentle love, like a feather's fall
As pleasant as the sound of a dove's call

A love as beautiful as a sunset
That stays as fresh as the day we met
A man that's passionate and full of fire
Who is able to fulfill my burning desire
A man who needs what I have to give
And wants to share in this life I live
This is my petition each time I pray
That this great love would come my way
I'm not asking for flawlessness
Only that God would grant me happiness

Alphabet of Knowledge

There's so much I have to give
And that I want to share
In this life that I live
With someone who will care

My aura, my anointing, my all
My beliefs, my best, my call

My character, my composure, my cheer
All that I hold dear

My ego, my failures, my fights
My flaws, my God, my heights

My intelligence, my jokes, my kiss
My love, my life, all I miss

My nakedness, my openness, my pride
My quips, my realness, my stride

My sexuality, my smile, my silence
My treasures, my unbelief, my violence

My wishes, my wiles, my will
My youth, my yearning and my zeal

I need someone to know all about me
Yet, continue to love me

Coming Together

When God does the choosing, the choice is right
This is why I hang on so tight
I always knew we would come together
That we would survive the stormy weather
That at some point in time we would find
What's ahead is better than what's behind

As I think back, I can so easily recall
All the things you've done for me, great and small
I can recollect the times that you were there
You didn't have to be and no one else would dare
Times I've hurt you because I didn't know
Exactly how you felt since you never let it show

In our present, it seems to be
Without you, there's no me
With each smile and every stolen kiss
It takes me closer to the place called bliss
And with each glance, one thing is sure
We have a love that will endure

I come closer to you and open my heart
Deciding this love will be my new start
I will refuse to worry, doubt or fear
But day by day, I will draw near
I'm am yours, entrusted to you
Take me now and do whatever you want to

Important That You Know

It's important that you know
Just how I feel
That since I've met you
I've began to heal
That because of your gentleness
I smile even in my sleep
You got to know
My feelings run deep

I appreciate your patience
And your tenderness with me
Your bountiful love
Sets me free

You are simply irresistible
An enticing treat
I would never hurt you
Nor lie or cheat

You are all that to me
I love you so
You can trust me, sweetheart
It's important that you know

Exercises of Faith

When there's nothing else to do
I sit here and believe for you
So far away and so long gone
On my face, I lie prone
Missing you more each passing day
Can only go on what you say
I turn to God for an answer for my friend
Hoping you can feel these prayers I send
Believing to have you in my life
Believing God to be your wife
Believing God to pull you near
Believing God to get you here
Believing God to set you free
Believing God, won't listen to me
I in myself am full of fear
Of losing a love I hold so dear
But the Christ in me will hold on to His Will
There is a destiny for you to fulfill
Faith is my substance to see you today
It's my evidence to lead the way
I miss you my love, my heart, my dream
Things are not as bad as they seem
You're coming home to your wife-to-be
God is going to move for me

Dedication

This is dedicated to the man I love
There are some things I want you to know

Do you suppose in your wonderings that I'll forget
Or that I will walk away
No matter how hard things get
I am here to stay

In your painful times, do you presume
I don't really care
You don't want to worry me, I assume
So you won't let me be there

If when you're hurting, I'm not around
It has nothing to do with you
There's something in this life I've found
It will always be true

That when times get rough
Real love won't run
No matter if the battle is tough
Love is about more than fun

Love isn't found in the words we say
It's found in what we do
Love doesn't fade with the passing of day
But is always dedicated to you

I love you, darling, and am dedicated to you
I just wanted you to know

The Great Exchange, His Part

Isn't it swell to fall in love
A most wonderful gift from above
To meet a man full of passion and romance
With whom I can share destiny's dance

Someone who can understand me from deep inside
Someone who won't take me for a ride
What a dream, to get roses, poems and candy
For no good reason, Oh, how dandy

For my man to actually listen to me
And care about what I see
I could love a man who tries hard to possess me
Not that he has to, but it would impress me

For a man to call me at midnight
Just to say he loves me and it will be alright
I could love a man who brings me breakfast in bed
This is a man I could wed

I could adore a man who trusts and confides in me
I believe this is how it really should be

The Great Exchange, My Part

What I wouldn't do for a man as such
I'd give him my love and compassion much
I'd shower him with affection all of his days
I'd blow his mind in many ways

Each day I would greet him with a kiss
Make sure when he's gone, it's me he'll miss
I would be his lover, his friend and his star
Our relationship would raise the bar

I would build him up, never tearing him down
On his face would never be a frown
He could have his way with all of me
More, more, more would be my plea

Whatever he wanted would not be denied
All of my devotion would be applied
I would keep his secrets and speak only good
I would treat him like a real woman should

As a queen gives herself to the king
My whole self I would often bring
To take his frustrations, pride and pain
To make him feel free again

The Unsuspecting Bride

Dedicated to my best friend, Kenna

What happens when a woman finds her dream
When things are not what they seem
Are we so superficial as to say
It has to be done only our way

When you came along
It was then I could see
You represented the greater side of me
It was you who brought rhythm to my rhyme

It was you who gave me back my life
You helped me to redeem the time
And rise above the strife
Unsuspecting, I walked into
What is now a dream come true

So with eyes hard closed
And my heart open wide
I throw away all my pride
I enter into something new
Something as great as the sun
Something that involves us two
I will no longer run

I quiet myself, and now I wait
As I'm the promised to be your mate

Night After Night

Night after night, gazing at the moon
I know our love was meant to be
With each day that passes, I need you more
Even so, I long for you as a desert longs for water

Night after night, looking into your eyes
I know there's no place I'd rather be
And with each passing instant
I'm ravished with your love

Night after night, watching you sleep
I fall more deeply in love with you
With each passing second
I want to be there to hold you

Night after night and day after day
I find myself with thoughts of only you
Moment by moment and time and again
You are all I desire out of life

I know you deserve the entire world
Please let it start with me
After years will have passed us by
I'll still be deeply in love with you

Night after night, I dream of you
Night after night, I need you
Night after night, I am yours alone

Your Essence

Each day as we're together, I become more like you
I take in, more and more, the essence of you

When you come home and your day has been long
For you I will remain strong
When all you need is me to minister to you
That's exactly what I will do

Each day I will cover you in prayer
And all your burdens I will share
As we lay together in the night
I won't say no or put up a fight

At the point of ecstasy, we become the same
Because we are married, there is no shame
Being your wife includes accepting your essence
There's no greater joy than being in your presence

Each time I see you, my heart still flutters
And when you kiss me, my brain still clutters
In your essence, I will continually relish
That you are a great man, no need to embellish

There's no part of me that I will ever withhold
In the greatest adversity, I will stand bold
I've become like you in so many ways
And will be with you all of my days

In the Position for Love

As eagerness seizes my soul
I anxiously await the day, my love
I position myself at the precipice of passion
Preparing myself for the leap of my life
As I explore the abyss of what lies ahead
I earnestly desire to improve
Technique after technique in book after book
I am positioning myself for love

Will you enjoy my kisses
Will you prefer my hugs
Will you relish my gentle touches
Will you savor and delight in my love
We choose to walk this through faith
Never knowing what prize lies inside the box
Will it be fulfilling, or will it blow my mind
Will we ever be the same

The day approaches, the moments are more intense
Your ardent love each day becomes more evident
Hugs leading to kisses and then to a caress
Sleepless nights abound as we imagine our love
Like Esther, I'm spending my time in preparation
In the position to receive and appreciate your love

First Kiss

There is something so delicate about that first time
Whether it is a soft brushing together of lips
Or a passionate exploration of the other's being
There is nothing that rivals the first kiss

The look that comes when a kiss is imminent
Our eyes lock and our hearts make a melody
In cadence we move together, closer and closer
Joining together in the dance of passion

At the point of our connection
And in concert with one another
Our lips touch gently but with enthusiasm
Discovering the fervor of anticipation fulfilled

The first kiss we shared was more of a journey
The beginning of intimacy and pleasure
Our first step over the boundaries of reality
Establishing a relationship through faith

The first kiss from my man of God
Left me panting for more of you in secret places
But I understand the power of expectation
The day of culmination will be more than a kiss

My Valentine

When I first met you, sweetheart
How can words express
From the first look into your eyes
I knew that you would be my valentine

The first touch of your lips on my cheeks
The first touch of your breath upon my face
I guess I always knew
You would be my valentine

Each time we're together
And you look into my soul
I bare myself before you
Only because you are my valentine

Don't ever leave me alone
Stay here with me always
Know that what we have is real
I'm dedicated to you only
My love for you will grow each day
And you will always be my valentine

Value

When he came into my life
With every intention of making me his wife
He never said how long he'd wait
Or how long he'd desired me for a mate

He only said he had heard a voice
Not really giving him a choice
That I was the one chosen to be
He'd get what he needed in me

And I knew that he was sure of what he heard
Because it was all centered around the Word
As time went on, I began to see
The value of prayer, bringing him to me

He was all I'd asked for in a man
A grand part of God's plan
He is full of destiny yet devoid of pride
And I will always be by his side

In his quiet way, he's provided relief
And has helped me come to the belief
That in the midnight hour, God is there
And of all our prayers, He is aware

Whether He moves quick, or does it slow
The value we put in our faith needs to grow
There is a definitive value in the wait
I've found that God is never late

Deeper

Amazing lover, let me delve deeper
Help me to see the inner you

Precious man of God, what would succeed
There is nothing in life to turn me away
There are no secrets that can destroy
What we share today

In all my devotion to you
No matter how painful your secrets may be
There is no doubt in mind
Being with you is my destiny

Let me know you in a private way
Let me see you, the good and the bad
Let me be the one to comfort you
Let me be your shoulder when you're sad

Deeper, together, I want us to go
And to get closer along the way
To share our disappointments with one another
No matter what anyone may say

Can I explore the depths of your soul
Let me get to know you
Amazing lover, let me delve deeper
Help me to see the inner you

Intimacy

Laying myself bare before you
It takes so much trust
It takes a certain kind of blindness
Even though in truth I can see
The closer I get to you
The deeper we go
The more vulnerable I become
But, it's in this vulnerability that I find intimacy

My confidence grows with the passing years
As I realize your love for me
Still, there are things you don't know about me
Does it feel as if I'm cheating you
There are some things only God knows
For me to try to explain it would be fruitless
Some parts of my life are only good for testimony
Why would I burden you with them

Intimacy is sharing what made me who I am
Intimacy is giving up my autonomy
Intimacy requires that I yield my secrets to you
Not always in words, but always through deeds
To show the things that I'll never say
To say the things that has never been said
Intimacy requires me to accept you into my heart
And leave myself unprotected

True intimacy requires total trust
And trust you I will

In the Bedroom

Hush, my darling, and relax tonight
Let me take you far away
I want to hold you tight
From the night until the day

Sweet and wonderful man of mine
This night will hold much pleasure
As our bodies intertwine
We'll experience ecstasy beyond measure

In the bedroom, I'll minister to you
And wash away your tears
There's no limit to what I will do
To eradicate your fears

As we lay together
I'm yours like never before
Through the most stormy weather
It'll always be you that I adore

In the bedroom, I yield to you
I lay down my will
I give myself to you
Because I trust you still

Precipice

Stand here with me
Let us see
How do we scale this wall

We are together
And as soft as a feather
We begin to fall

Over the cliff of fantasy
And as it should be
It doesn't hurt at all

As you embrace me
And turn to face me
I can hear your voice call

At the precipice of peace
I find a release
To give you my all

To Receive

Growing up and changing each day
Will live in victory, come what may
Refusing to settle for anything less
Living by revelation, no longer have to guess

Doing what I must to receive you
Chosen as God's gift to you
Will humble myself and seek His Will
Teaching myself to be still

Preparing my temple for what is holy
Giving myself to one man wholly
As weeks turn to months and them to years
I will cherish each day, whether of smiles or tears

With my eyes on you, I pass my test
Giving up the old to receive God's best
This is a place where provisions never cease
In God's will, there is an abundance of peace

Yes, and truly, I believe
I'm more than ready to receive

Act 8

A New Beginning

Whispers of My Heart

Filled with a dream that is yet to exist
Awaiting the daylight's sun
Hollowed out on the inside
Preparing myself to run

Chasing a promise spoken with unseen lips
But convinced in my mind
That the dream, the promise and the promiser
Are not that hard to find

There is a whisper in my heart
It leads me along the way
It grants me wisdom and prosperity
As long as I will obey

This whisper gives me peace
So that I know my path is right
This whisper often envelopes me
And pulls me toward the light

In the whispers of my heart
My strength is sustained
So that through faith and trust
My dream is obtained

Becoming

Before I was considered a saint
I was called a sinner
Before I became a woman of God
And before I became a winner
I was still becoming…

Evolution of a woman
As she is becoming…

Long before I knew of God
He was thinking of me
Years before the transformation began
He already knew who I would be

Evolution of a woman
As she is becoming…

Am I becoming pretty, beautiful or gorgeous
Am I becoming virtuous, patient or kind
Will I be the epitome of honor
And a breed that's hard to find

Am I becoming a woman of God
Full of his wisdom and grace
Will I be all the things He desires
Will I see His image in my face

Evolution of a woman
As she is becoming…

What Is Woman

The beauty of her hands
The softness of her voice
The touch of her lips
Let nature run its course

She never fails to be there for you
There's no end to her dedication
She wakes up at the break of day
She is full of determination

A quiet strength
She is gentle and kind
She knows when to submit
But still has her own mind

She can stand under pressure
Her shoulders are strong
She is always on your side
But will tell you when you are wrong

A woman, a gift, what a awesome treat
The woman, her life, love that can't be beat
A woman, her emotions, who can understand
The woman, your woman, God's gift to man

Rapturous Delight

The seasons change with much ado
With dramatic transitions
Each new days brings us closer
To the era of timelessness

With the rushing of clouds and time that flies
Often, it's our life we defer forgetting the One
One that's seen only in secret places
And whose knowing is found only in eternity
Here and there are the warning signs
In our busyness, we pass them by

Engulfed in transitory cocoons
Only to come out unchanged where it counts
Then a shockingly great surprise
The rapture of sweet delight

Who will go to join in the dance
And who will watch the same
Like a wall flower, are we planted
Or like a breeze, will we float

Will we meet in the air with our coming Prince
Or shall we ever be awaiting the fantasy of return
Shall we dance heartily to the beat of a heavenly drum
Or will we, as so many nights before, remain in the realm
of impossibilities!

To Change

Filled with contradictions and insecurities
My life is full of uncertainties
Survived poverty, but will I survive wealth
Made it through sickness to have health

Took a lot of bad while searching for the good
Now that it's here, will I behave as I should
My heart grew stronger in the times of pain
And learned to rely on God in times of rain

There were many times my heart was broken
And so many words went unspoken
I've cried myself to sleep many nights
People have infringed upon all my rights

And now that life is improving for me
I wonder if fortune will change how I see
Now that I possess all that I need
Will I continue to allow God to lead

In this season, it's my heart I search
My answers won't be found in a church
But deep within, I must know what's true
And what God expects me to do

To Change, Part 2

I must have an encounter in my heart
So my God and I will never be apart
I must look deeply to find what's hiding there
And lay it all before Him, open and bare

Whatever my encounter does uncover
I can leave it in the hands of my Lover
My Jesus, my God, my faithful friend
For all that's broken, He can mend

It must be Him to keep me
And make me what I need to be
In all my doubts about my humanity
There is one certainty

He is sovereign and knows all my flaws
And who picks me up after all my falls
Rags or riches, with Him I will stay
Wealth has a tendency to fly away

My health may not always last
Beauty may become a thing of the past
But I trust Him in all His ways
I leave in His hands all my days

Looking at my heart, I finally see
God has really changed me

Inspired

Nature's beauty, God's grand design
No improvements to what is fine
Of all the most beautiful things to ever be desired
The work of God's hands makes me feel inspired

Autumn's color and spring's smell
The flow of water we know so well
Of all the most beautiful things to ever be desired
The work of God's hands makes me feel inspired

Summer's heat and winter's cold
Never useless even though it's old
Of all the most beautiful things to ever be desired
The work of God's hands makes me feel inspired

The body of a man, sculptured to perfection
Never in need of a human's correction
Of all the most beautiful things to ever be desired
The work of God's hands makes me feel inspired

Though there's plenty to admire
And when time seems to expire
And the wicked begin to perspire
And there's nothing left in life to desire
Only God can inspire

My Grandmother's Eyes

The eyes staring back at me
Doesn't even belong to me
I see my grandmother's eyes

My reflection keeps changing
And day to day
I find myself in metamorphosis
The old me dying away

And in my process, my vision is changed
I see myself with an open mind
It seems I no longer see like me
To my faults, I'm going blind

My grandmother's eyes saw me in purity
They often saw me whole
Sometimes they saw me hurting
Even piercing through my soul

As I look at myself
I study my reflection
All I see is Annie's eyes
Full of love and affection

Reunited

I take a walk to a far away village
I smell my grandma's cookies
Too long gone to bake and to laugh
But not long enough to cry
I wrestle with the urge to stop and speak

I'm at the steps
I'm at the door
I turn around and there's my grandma
Grandma's smell and grandma's smile
Grandma's scar and grandma's hair

I go with my grandma
She takes me by my hand
She talks to me and laughs at me
We walk for hours and never tire
Then I see it for the first time

A castle in the sky, walking on gold streets
Reunited with my grandma in Jerusalem

Suspended

Suspended on faith
Nothing else around
This is the place
Where dreams are found

By the words of His mouth
Power will descend
By His truth
Hearts will mend

Majesty and splendor
You are wonderful and great
When I need you
You're never too late

Excellency and Savior
Who you are to me
I'm here by your grace
It's plain to see

I can't see you
But I know you're here
I'm in love with you
Because you're always near

Faith works by love
And this we share
Turning from everything
I haven't a care
I am suspended on faith

Act 9

God's Word to Us

Let Me Love You

I can hear His heart's cry
Let me love you, my child
Can you imagine it
Close your eyes

Let me love you the way only I can
There is no replacement to be found in man
Let me give you all you need
Let me impregnate you with my seed

Let me show you the way to me
Helping you to be all you can be
Come away with me from this place
Set the atmosphere and seek my face

Let me love you and keep you secure
In my faithfulness, you can be sure
Let my love saturate you
Let me be there in all you do

Can you hear the cry of a father's heart
Our insensitiveness is tearing Him apart
Let Him love you, you won't regret it
This is His heart, don't ever forget it

Exhortations

For The Ministry God Has Given Me

Just in case you forgot what Jesus said
Excuses are the opposite of what you've read
Stand up, be responsible, He died for you
Uncover yourself, His love is true

Seems our Savior has done it all
Still, sometimes, we manage to fall
Through all the heartache, He was there
Instead of turning away, He was aware
Loving us through all the faults inside
Leading us closely as we begin to die

Savior, all I need and more
You are the wings that make me soar
Verily I say unto you
Escape the pain of what you do
Still, Jesus Saves!

Don't Just Be

It isn't enough to just be who you are
Someone is always looking at you
To someone, you are a star
It doesn't matter what you do

Be careful of your deeds
Your legacy is at stake
Meet other's needs
Live for Christ's sake

Don't just be who they tell you to be
You were created with purpose in mind
No matter what others see
Leave their opinions behind

Don't just be simple or plain
You were designed to do great things
All the sacrifice isn't in vain
Nor the joys that sacrifice brings

Don't just be alive but enjoy your life
Don't allow it to pass you by
Through salvation, let go of the strife
And never be afraid to try

What Is Life

What is a life if not pain and pleasure
What in life do you treasure
Is it your freedom and the right to exist
Or are they hard to narrow from your long list

If so, you're fortunate and that indeed
Many have lives full of need
From the need for food to the need for water
To missing the presence of the Father

We often ignore the cries we hear
Because we value our lives all too dear
Everybody wants to smile and none to cry
But for every one of our lives someone had to die

His name was Jesus and He died for us all
In the midst of His shame, he stood tall
Freedom isn't free and life isn't cheap
There is nothing here we get to keep

All we can do is to do our part
That is helping others from the heart
So what is life if not pleasure and pain
And the wealth of experience we can gain

Larry and Dean

Laying in the sunshine
Always smiling with hope
Really not to sure about tomorrow
Really don't care
You have to be able to move on

By tears and pain
Real life makes itself known
As I look around
Days seem to pass in a moment
For this reason am I happy
Only because now I know
Realness is the good and the bad
Desire brings them both

Desert thoughts of yesterday
Embrace a new tomorrow
Always remember your God
Never wallow in your sorrow

Cry, Cry

My friend is heart sick
So many things going on
Too many pains for one to pick
Yet he tries to be strong
Eye to eye
All he can do is cry, cry

Death of family, awaken to grief
Hurting in the night
Catastrophe steps in like a thief
Nothing seems to go right
Looking in his eyes
All I see is cries, cries

Cry my love, cry out my friend
I will hold your hand
God will let no more pain come in
He will take a stand
Cry, cry
Let out the grief
Cry, cry
And find your relief

Balm

I am the balm of Gilead
In me find your healing
No need to walk around sad
All you need to be is willing

In this balm is abundance of peace
And a time for us to share
A time for you to increase
And release all your care

In the balm that I provide
I know you can be whole
All your issues will subside
And you'll have peace to your soul

Come, my child, receive your balm
Don't let it pass you by
Let my love bring you calm
Let me be there when you cry

I am the balm of Gilead
In me find your healing
No need to walk around sad
All you need to be is willing

Glimpse into Glory

Take a glimpse into glory
Let me tell you my story

Ever existing throughout the ages
Us three with none other beside
In companionship with one another
In a place devoid of pride

Then we created angels in the heavens
Their purpose was to praise our name
They were faithful over their duties
Then that fateful day came
The one, my favorite, did rebel
Lifting himself against me
He even encouraged others to join him
In his revolt against me

In my glory and my great love
I spared him for a season
Knowing one day the time would come
I would finally have a reason
Then in my desire for fellowship
I created you
It's my very breath of life
That sustains you

But because of you, I can say
I wouldn't have it any other way

Lifter of Your Head

Take a breath, what do you feel
And who undergirds you
For you I'm filled with a great zeal
I'll always be here for you

When you shed all your tears
Just remember I bottle every one
Even in your darkest years
You're in the hands of my Son

When you feel like I've forgotten
Remember your name is engraved in my hand
I even gave up my only begotten
I hope you can understand

I've loved you with an everlasting affection
I'll never give up on you
Please don't faint when I send correction
It matters to me what you do

I've made myself the lifter of your head
And your battle axe too
Until the day your body is dead
I'll never abandon you

Even then my love will follow you where it is led
Please, let me always be the lifter of your head

The Holy Place

Come dine with me, my chosen vessel
Allow me to search you through
Dive into the abyss with me
Trust me, I'll protect you

Come into the sacred place
Come prepared to seek my face
I'll give you power to run this race
And cover you always in my grace

As you endeavor to please me
Don't forget where you're going
It takes power to live this life
It takes a lot of growing

Your growth comes from fellowship
With me and my Son
There's no other way to get it
When all is said and done

Come into the sacred place
Come prepared to seek my face
I'll give you power to run this race
And cover you always in my grace

*****

Moment of Reflection

This is my life: the good, the bad, and the not so bad. I've loved hard. I've lost big. I've suffered much. I've had grief and sorrow. By the same token, I've been loved. I've won. I've grown and blossomed into a woman of God. Does the end justify the means? Yes, it does. It unequivocally does.

A friend once told me that my life is what movies are made of. It's been an extraordinary life. It's been full of sun and rain. I can only imagine what my future holds. At this point in my life, the one thing I'm sure of is that God holds my destiny. I know that when the bad comes, it will be for my purging, for my growth and for my making. I know that when the good comes, it will be for the glory of God. I know that when I'm blessed, it is to be a blessing to someone else. I know that when I struggle, it's to turn me from the world and to God.

In your reading, I pray you found that God is always in control. When we fall short, when we are in pain, when we are in turmoil, when we doubt, God is still in control. When the hard times seem to outweigh the good times, God is in control. When I lost what I thought was the love of my life, it turned for my good. Now I'm engaged to one of the most awesome men of God in the world. He is my friend and my confidante. God sent him. Had I gotten what I wanted, I would have missed what I needed. God is good!

I pray you were touched and your circumstances were put into perspective. God hasn't forgotten you. He loves you and won't forsake you, even when you're at your lowest point.

~Lacresha~

Printed in the United States
109965LV00001B/217-318/A

9 780979 815430